Out of Body

to

Hell

by

BEVERLY J. WILLIAMS, DM

Mgi

✵

Out of Body to Hell

A Crystal Clear Love Warning

Copyright © 2024, 2004 by Beverly J. Williams
Printed in the United States of America
Library of Congress Control Number: 2024924846
ISBN-13: 978-1-889552-12-5
ISBN-10:   1-889552-12-7

No part of this book may be reproduced, stored, or transmitted in any form by any means without prior written permission of the author/publisher except for brief reviews for publications. All rights reserved under International and/or United States of America Copyright Law(s). No excessive remittance for book distributions.

This Memoir is based on the author's own, personal, experiences regarding hell as witnessed by her in 2003. It is intended to expose the reality of the events to the masses; and, be a tool to assist in the ministries of the people of the Lord God. It is for informational, educational, inspirational, and spiritual purposes. Neither Author nor Publisher is responsible nor liable for any misinterpretations.

ISBN-13: 978-1-889552-14-9 (eBook, elec./digital, oob2h, Eng, 02/2026)
ISBN-13: 978-1-889552-07-1 (paper, 5.25 x 3.5, erss, Span., 05/2004)
ISBN-13: 978-1-889552-06-4 (paper, 5.25 x 3.5, hrhs, 02/2004, 12/2003)

Unless otherwise noted, all Scripture is from the King James Version and the New King James Version of the Holy Bible of God.

Cover text and interior layout by Beverly J. Williams. Cover background with permission. If inspired and support this Ministry, Thank you. May God return it 100-fold (Mark 10:30).

Ministers of the Gospel, Inc. *(Mgi)*
PO Box 277 ~ Haskell, OK 74436   *(www.ms7.com)*

First Edition, Eighth Printing   *Selah*✶

i ~ Dedication

With humble submission, this Literary Proclamation is dedicated to You, my LORD God and heavenly Father; to You, Christ Jesus, my King and only Potentate; to You, Holy Ghost, my Comforter: You know, see, hear, speak, ... Supreme over every thing!!! (Psalm 148)

***TO** you, my husband, yours and mine together— the time. Your always welcoming strength, surrounding protection, devoted love, listening ear— being here! I am grateful to God.*
"they shall be one" (Gen .2:24b)

"He that has an ear, let him hear what the Spirit says to the churches." (Rev. 3:22).

"Come up here, and I will show you things which must be hereafter. And immediately I was in the spirit: and, behold, a throne was set in heaven, and One sat on the throne." (Rev. 4:1b-2)

✷

Contents

i	Dedication	iii
ii	Acknowledgments	vii
iii	Foreword	ix
iv	Love Warning	x
v	Introduction	xi

~ Out of Body to Hell ~

1.	Out of Body to Hell	1
2.	Beginning	2
3.	Judgment	3
4.	The Descent	7
5.	Reasons	9
6.	Arrival	15
7.	Torments	29
8.	I Came Back	35
9.	Finality	45
10.	Addendum	48
11.	Questions & Answers	49
12.	Definitions	56
13.	God's Word to Us	58
14.	Epilogue	60
15.	Pray Aloud	62
16.	Endnotes ✳	63
17.	Notes	70
18.	About the Author	72
19.	Literary, Digital, Media	73
20.	Scan QR Code	74

ii ~ **Acknowledgments**

Thank You LORD God, my Inspiration; omniscient, omnipresent, omnipotent, eternal God.

Thank you to:

My tenacious husband, Dr. Floyd W. Williams, Sr., a man of 'great faith'—my hero. *(Mat. 8:10)*

Min. Marie (Lang) Wilson, my diligent and genuinely selfless, interior sketches illustrator *(12)*.

My unwavering circle of God's effectual, fervent, prayer warriors, intercessors, and saints—you did not give up on me—but stayed *(warred! the kingdom of heaven suffers violence, and the violent take it by force [Mat. 11:12])*! You know who you are, God does also. We win—that others may be FREE!

All, for opening your various ministries, studios, broadcast media; you missionaries, nations, translators, distributors, encouragers; financial supporters *(every penny went toward more books, may God return it to you 100-fold. Mark.10:30)*; others who helped get this Love Warning out—too many to name, we're in this together. To GOD be all the glory!!!

"Hi There—thank you for reading this book! As you journey through these pages, I pray you will discover each one enlightening! I believe this clear Love Warning will reveal the information you seek. *In Jesus' name. Amen!*" ✷

iii ~ **Foreword**

The doctrine of hell is Biblical and can be uncomfortable for most of us, but Jesus talked frequently about it in the Gospels.

I believe that Dr. Beverly J. Williams had a real experience in that place of eternal torment; and that, she described it in this book in great detail.

She references with various Scripture that aids the reader in using this book as a wonderful study guide.

May this experience that she describes explicitly warn multitudes of people; and, encourage them to make JESUS the LORD of their soul and thereby, live eternally in heaven.

—Pastor Colleen Litsey
Anchor of Hope

✶

iv ~ **Love Warning**

This book should be read by young and old as a warning from God. I found myself repenting of every sin that would keep me out of heaven.

Dr. Beverly has made it clear through this book that, whoever rejects Christ as Lord, are people who have made their own choice to go to hell. Hell was only designed for Satan and his fallen angels.

As a Minister, Evangelist, and Directress of the Great White Throne Judgment Ministry *(GWT)*, I take this very seriously.

—Evangelist Mollie Robbins, Directress
Great White Throne Judgment
Ministries (GWT)

✶

v ~ **Introduction**

"Momma, don't worry about me, I'll be okay. I'm going to grow up to be a good lady like you want me to be. I'm going to marry somebody that's really good. I'll be okay."

When I was conceived, my parents weren't quite ready. They were going through changes when my mother found herself expecting the last of five. Also during that era, it wasn't thought safe to have a child if the mother was over age 35. In her predicament, she became very afraid. Someone offered to loan her money to get an abortion—she refused to do that.

Very concerned, she depended on prayer during and after the pregnancy. Her requests were that God take care of me and allow her to live until I could take care of myself.

During one of her prayers, and my toddler age, I offered her comfort with the above statement.

[Note: When book published, Mom was 85, Dad was 87.]

I found the big family Bible—yes, ours had dust on it too. While cooking, Mom recited to me its contents from memory as I pretended I was reading it.

Who am I? I was pretty much considered the good girl. The one through High School branded, "Goodie two-shoes." Though already walking in it, I'd accepted my call to ministry decades ago and have continued steadfast.

I am a Christian. People ask whether I'm Pentecostal, Baptist, Methodist, this or that? "No!" I follow after the LORD God through Jesus Christ my heart's love. *(Acts 11:26; I Peter 4:16; I Corinthians 1:12-13)*

I've taught the Bible to other cultures, ministered on skid row, in correctional facilities, street rallies, retreats, seminars, conferences, as co-interim pastor for churches, authored a few books, provided tapes, CDs, whatever God would have me do. I've tried to be obedient. (Some books to countries. Now audio & eBooks).

There's a great shifting taking place. I believe God is giving ethnic groups across the universe various revelatory experiences of what's occurring in the

INTRODUCTION

spirit-realm. He is preparing something across the globe and we need to be sober, awake, and ready with oil in our lamps.

I believed the experiences of those who died or got shot and said they went to hell; but, when that thing (the experience to hell) happened to me, it was a whole interesting reality. I knew something very big was happening with the Christian community in this world today.

What was I doing going to hell?! Some accounts I'd heard seemed to include a sinful life. Well, I believe in Jesus, that He's the only begotten Son of God, who died for our sins, rose again, and is seated at the right hand of the Father. I believe the Scriptures, try to live right, mean what I say, and do unto others as I would have them do unto me. *(St. Matthew 7:12)*

Some ask, "Why do you think this happened to you?" I can tell you what I think (see infra Questions & Answers).

Oh yes, by-the-way, God did let me marry a good man, Floyd W. Williams, Ph.D., my beloved husband of decades. To me, he exemplifies Christianity as more than a conqueror in Christ Jesus. "MINISTERS OF THE GOSPEL" with emphasis in teaching; we are <u>not</u> evangelists (though our work includes evangelism. *II Timothy 4:5*). The LORD God bless and keep you.

*<u>Note</u>: "But against any of the children of Israel shall not a dog move his tongue, against man or beast: that you may know <u>how</u> that **the LORD <u>does</u> put a difference** between the Egyptians and Israel." Ex.11:7*

*

INTRODUCTION

OUT OF BODY TO HELL

1 ~ **Out of Body to Hell** ~

"This place looks familiar," I heard my being say. Just entering my bedroom door, I turned back to again recognize it, my closet, then my dresser. "What am I doing here? Why am I back here?" I was afraid that actually, I was still in hell, and **was dreaming** that I was out of hell.

On the morning of August 19, 2003, about 8:00 a.m., I came to myself. I **thought** it was a dream. I told my husband, "I dreamt—I went—to hell." Nonetheless, some who know about things like that told me I had an out-of-body experience. **WHAT**?! Who could I talk to? Who could I tell? I needed somebody to talk to me!

I've always been a dreamer.[1] God has allowed me to have many dreams, visions, and experiences[2] about heaven, the rapture, and other things; BUT—oh my God! this one was **the biggie**. This one is the inspiration for this entire book![3]   ✳

2 ~ **Beginning**

Months just preceding the New Year 2003, I heard the Lord calling[4] me saying, "Come here baby, come here. I want you to sit down. I want to talk to you." I began telling my husband, "Honey, I'm hearing God say, 'Come here,' and I need to go."[5] It was time to take another, what I call, "sabbatical."[6]

During such times, I do necessary things, omit unnecessary things, and spend increased quality time with the Father; but this time, I wasn't even allowed to accept ministerial speaking engagements.

Consequently, my dreams and visions became more vivid and most intense to the degree it seemed I was actually in them; and upon awaking, as if I'd been to the places.

✱

3 ~ **Judgment**

"And as it was in the days of Noah, so it will be also in the days of the Son of Man"

(St. Luke 17:26-30)

I was inside my home, going about my daily activities; just like everyone else, whatever they do. I'm typically trying to hear from God. Trying to get **my** spiritual life right.[7] Trying to grow in the things of the Lord because people are hurting and looking for real food. They need someone to truly talk to,[8] someone who's real, and will be there for them. This calls for sacrificial living.

Suddenly I floated, then immediately noticed I was outside. I saw many I know of and associate with: all the pastors, preachers, teachers, evangelists, apostles, bishops, prophets, deacons, leadership, laity, churchgoers,[9] proclaimed saints, believers, ministry workers, relatives, all of us, whatever we call ourselves,[10] simultaneously floating—hovering 2-3 feet off of the earth! (Psalm 90:10; Jer. 23:11, 20-21)

Structures were transparent or not there.[11] I had clear unobstructed vision across the span of the universe. I noticed myriads of others[12] elevated in like manner. We did not go above the trees.

We floated[13] toward the west (not the east[14] from which Jesus will come) very easily and slowly. It was as if each of us were being carried by our collar with the thumb and forefinger of one angel[15] per person. Like one carrying the filthiest handkerchief[16] to be added to the dirty clothes basket. (Ez.8:3b, 13:3, 6, 20) Time was no more. (Rev. 10:6, 11:18)

As we were floating, the sky and ground turned from light to grey, dark grey to black, then very black[17] until we arrived over an area black as tar.[18]

Seeing the clouds change I thought, "Oh my God! I'm going to hell?!"[19] I was in total shock, total dismay, terrified. I knew there was no turning back,[20] nothing I could do about it.

JUDGMENT

We weren't tossed or thrown but simply released[21] like "yucck," not to have to be remembered. I was later impressed that the filthy handkerchief description represented our righteousness as filthy rags.[22]

But! I didn't want-to-go to hell! I was shocked![23] That indicates to me that, some who believe with all their heart they're going to heaven, **will be shocked** if they find themselves on their way to hell.[24]

They won't believe they're going to hell! Many will believe they did many **mighty works in Jesus' name**; but actually, were[25] workers of iniquity.[26] Perhaps with incorrect motives, for gain, or flamboyancy.[27] Such is unacceptable. Many say, "I **know** the Lord!" but the key is, does the Lord **know** them? (Mat. 7:23)

Though we call Jesus, "Lord,"[28] it depends on whether or not the true meaning of "**Lord**" is resident and being exercised in addressing Him. Not when one uses His title merely to express disappointment, and never as a sincere term of endearment.

Some will be judged according to **their works**—those things found written in "the books."[29] Works include physical, and works (intentions) of the heart.[30] God tries the reins of our hearts.[31]

Myriads of Scripture tell us how[32] to recognize when one may be headed for the gates[33] of hell; e.g., by their fruits you will know them (Mat. 7:20); not choosing life;[34] those who **hear** the word, but not **do** the word (Mat. 7:26-27); blind leaders of the blind (Mat. 15:13-14); heart not right in sight of God (Acts 8:20-24); a son of the devil (Acts 13:10). "Consequently, **people** make their beds in hell."[35]

✶

4 ~ **The Descent**

I began descending slowly, very easily, down, down, down,[36] along with all of these people I knew, and others. Everything was dark, black, and nasty. It was horrible, like being in the most filthiest pipe in your house. (Matt. 13:26-30, 38-43, 49-51)

I started getting warm, very warm, hot, then very hot![37] I saw crude, sludge, guck and blackness along the walls and corridors of the passage.[38] Every now and again, it seemed the crude[39] and sludge masses were little demons[40] embedded and sprinkled intermittently in the walls[41] of this massive container.

Like an unwilling magnet, my spiraling[42] disagreed with its fair-and-square surrender. This activity of descending was a natural, physiological phenomenon.[43] It was frightfully strange. It was unusual. I was floating?! downward?! and the presence of the others[44] was eminent.

∗

5 ~ Reasons

While descending, I had total, precise **knowledge of everything!**[45] It was my reality check; exceedingly keen, like magnified rhema! I wonder if it was relative to "the knowledge of evil" in Genesis 2:17? I knew every single reason I was going down there. Nobody had to tell me anything. I knew what I did and didn't do. **We'll know**[46] **why** we go!

The reason[47] I went was lumped in one: "I didn't hear[48] the Lord, I didn't heed[49] the Lord, I didn't receive the Lord; I, therefore, **did not do**[50] what the Lord said—but, I DID hear the Lord but, I **IGNORED**[51] Him!"

OUT OF BODY TO HELL

***"I was there!*[52] *I was talking to you!"*[53] resounded in me.

Wait-a-minute! even in Scripture! **Jesus came** in the volume of "The Book!"[54] I didn't get the magnitude!

My God, Jesus DID keep saying, "**He who has an ear, let him "hear!"**"[55] Also our communication was by knowledge![56] Why didn't I do it?! I didn't because I thought, "I'll do it like, later (procrastination);[57] when I get ready." Though not in a nasty vein, it was very easy!

Well, He told me. He told ALL of us![58] He just didn't **bang-it** over my head. So, I didn't accept it. Mostly, it WAS that **still, small, gentle voice**[59] we hear all the time!

REASONS

Now that I'm back, I know that's a reason lot's of people are down there right now. Jesus **DID** indicate, He **DID** tell us, in various ways. He told the whole world, the universe—ALL OF US!!![60]

Jeremiah 2:13 states: My people have committed two evils: 1) they have forsaken Me, the fountain of living waters; and, 2) hewn (made) themselves cisterns (receptacles, tanks)—broken cisterns that can hold no water.

God departed from King Saul who: 1) did not obey the voice of the Lord; and, 2) did not execute God's wrath upon Amalek (I Sam.28:15, 18).

Eternal life depends on whether or not one knows the Father and Jesus.[61] II Thess. 1:8 states: vengeance will be taken on those who: 1) do not know God, and, 2) **DO NOT OBEY** the gospel of Jesus.

"**Know**" means to perceive, understand, recognize, be acquainted, aware of the truth of, possessing confidential information of.

Jesus illustrated that **if** Peter loved Him, he'd take care of what belongs to Him (sheep).[62] Jesus entrusted the care of His mother to one of His beloved.[63] Both disciples WORKED for Jesus!

"**Obey**" means listen, hearken, heed, yield; humble acceptance of the Gospel; continuous subjection of faith under the preached word; keeping the word in believing obedience.

Philippians 2:12 states, as you have always obeyed, work out your own salvation with fear and trembling. (See Exodus 24:7) We ought to get busy.

Philippians 2:13 states, it's **God that works** in you both to will and DO His good pleasure. If God works (Gen. 1:1-2:3; John 19:30; Rev. 10:7), aren't we to be like minded and love Him enough to DO[64] His will? "For this is the love of God, that we keep His commandments" (I John 5:3).

Without faith, it's impossible to please God.[65] Faith is belief with corresponding action (works). Faith without works is dead (James 2:14, 17, 26).

It has been stated, we're not saved **because** we do good works, we do good works **because** we **are** saved! (Eph. 2:8-9)

James showed his faith **by** his works (James 2:18). Jesus was able to SEE the faith of men who uncovered a roof and lowered one to receive healing.[66]

OUT OF BODY TO HELL

6 ~ **Arrival**

When I arrived at some particular area[67] down there, immediately I saw white people, black people, an assortment of young people.[68] "Yes, young[69] people were there!" I also saw or perceived those who obey the local "murder demons,"[70] they were there; and the souls of some murdered[71] by them[72]—all were down there.

The people I saw looked just like we do right now![73] I saw the color of their pigmentation, their hair, their eyes: but the eyes did look very weird, like maybe terminal sockets.

It was like a dungeon[74] down there, with feces and its smell (as the existence of its combined dread) all over the place.

No light,[75] but I could see.[76] I could hear screams, but couldn't hear screams. I could "see" screams,[77] then couldn't. I saw mouths opening, but saw them closed. I heard screams and saw mouths open, then saw mouths closed, yet still heard the screams. There were echoes of delayed voices. My God! Hell is distorted, contorted, confused, inverted, perverted, nothing like it is here on earth!

Constantly, I had the feeling that, the worst[78] thing that could ever happen to me, was going to happen! I felt that with great grief; like a detriment, and in detriment. I went through a lot. The decay[79] in my body was sucking it in and out. All kinds of things happened.

Your worst fear, or the thing you feel most detestable about here on earth, meets[80] you down there—**whatever it is**! So you eternally exist in fear.

I wondered if this was **something** like what Jesus experienced but greater, since He **took** (received in Himself) away **ALL** the sins[81] of the ENTIRE WORLD!!!

I was shocked I went to hell! But what got me was, all these other people:[82] pastors, preachers, teachers, evangelists, apostles, bishops, prophets, deacons, lea-

ARRIVAL

dership, lay persons, churchgoers, proclaimed saints, believers, ministry workers, etc., we all went!

I saw the description[83] of a man who immediately grabbed me and began taunting me over and over, and with others, who were taunting[84] the rest of us. We couldn't run, but were trying to shake them off like, "Uh uh, get away!" We were defenseless[85]—they wouldn't move—there was no rescue at all![86]

The man who grabbed me took my head, put it on as if a guillotine, took a big hammer with a humongous hammerhead,[87] and started **banging my head** with it.[88]

"Aaaaaaah!!!" I hollered and screamed. I could feel all the excruciating pain, agony, degradation, grief, fear,[89] everything! and I knew—I could do nothing about it.

It seemed my head would cave in, but wouldn't cave in, or wouldn't stay caved in, or would spring back to shape. Consequently, he could repeatedly do this to me forever!

It was like, "Oh! you need someone to **bang-it** over your head?! Alright, we'll bang-it over your head." There was decay[90] in my body and in his, but they wouldn't decay; yet, they were decaying.

I was attacked, accosted, assaulted, violated, beat up, stressed, molested, hurt, mistreated, slandered, hit, accused, misused, abused. My heart, my brain were being molested. Someone can molest your baby finger and, MO-LEST it!

It was the worst of the worst. "Hope? what's that?! I could hear the others hollering and screaming,[91] but I couldn't reach back to help them, and they couldn't help me.[92]

The ones bothering us were themselves being tormented but worse than they were tormenting us. The ones tormenting the ones that were tormenting us, were themselves being tormented by others that were tormenting them worse than they were tormenting. It was like a business, with a manual vengeance, labor assembly line down there.

Seeing and experiencing such abundant mal-activity is when I noticed how exceedingly colossal (large) hell[93] is!

Demonic activity was loose and free, we were in their territory. The space we used, our existence there, helped make up the place of hell. It was like, we **belonged** down there (our just reward)![94]

The worst atrocities of the earth-realm are multiplied in hell. It's like, they **are** hell, the food in hell. They exist, thrive, grow, are rooted in, and are the feast of hell! All of the worst adjectives from "A-Z" live in hell.

I also saw hideous and torturous **film characters** down there. At this point, my knowledge revealed that sometimes, some movie producers have contact with the underworld through various mediums.[95]

They replicate and transport certain information, foul spirits,[96] profanity, deplorable and suggestive activities into TV and film. We watch the scary, seductive,[97] exploitative, blatantly disobedient,[98] witchcraft, addictive, pornographic, insulting, rebellious, overbearing, intrusive, violent programming. We feed its immoral influence to ourselves, as well as allow it to baby-sit our children.

Such programming enters our souls through our ear-gates, eye-gates,[99] senses. We inadvertently help release it into the earth–realm, licensing it to operate as "full-circle." Residing in flesh, it can take souls straight to hell. (2 Pet. 2:11)

As a result, we sometimes consequently hear of cruel crimes committed that appear identical to an action-packed portrayal in a film. Or, we'll notice our Li'l Boo-Bah prancing him or herself around in an extremely unseemly manner,[100] then we have the nerve to question, "Where **in-the-world**[101] such movements came from?" (I'd ask, "Which world did they come from?")

"Where there's no revelation, the people cast off their restraint "   *(Prov. 29:18)*

Some of it is calculated[102]—intended to destroy righteous ways of life. Eternal damnation (its full-circle destination) is where unrighteous ways have to go.

I did sense "**the Bliss**" (heaven) "up there"[103] somewhere; but I was way down there! I couldn't see the Bliss,[104] I had keen knowledge it existed. Knowledge of it was the most excruciating thing ever! I couldn't reach it, touch it, taste it, smell it. I couldn't communicate with anybody.

I didn't hope for the Bliss, because "**no hope**" is down there. No-no you see to me, there seems to be such a thing! It's like "a body" or, "an entity" (barrier) whose existence is NO HOPE! It's like its' name is, "No Hope"; yet, it consists a vast reality. So, you can't have hope, to hope. Therefore, I didn't intentionally cry, "Oh help!" for something I knew I wasn't going to get.

There's nothing there: no pity, no justice, no relief, no rescue, no hope. It's not like, "Okay, she's had enough."

OUT OF BODY TO HELL

Judgment (Heb. 9:27; Rev. 11:18a) had already been made, we were there, and sentencing was being carried out!

We were routinely[105] shifted and shuffled like cattle through other horrible corridors. Other nasty disdainful things were being done to us, just whatever: pushed, beat up, hit, inflicted, set on fire, choked trampled, squeezed, invaded, violated, exposed, harassed, scared, chided, jeered.

ARRIVAL

There were growlings, howlings,[106] beatings like frustrations being taken out on another. It reminded me of concentration camps and slavery quarters where people were whipped, spat on, hair shaved off, stripped naked, cold, improperly fed, sprayed with hoses, pushed down, restrained, forced, maligned, reproached, buffeted, etc.

The most hideous things one could do: decapitate, mutilate, or skin someone alive, it's all down there and worse!

When I arrived to the next corridor, I saw another man. He had a great big sledge hammer. He swung it back with great fervency; with rapid momentum it came toward me and, "Aaaaaaah!!!" It hit from the bottom of my chin to the bottom of my abdomen.

Again, my annihilated body wouldn't really annihilate. So, he could keep hitting me. It horrified me with unbearable, slicing pain (Ooooh!) again, and again, and again.

The first man was very gruff, mean, nasty looking, and simply detestable. I don't use the word, "ugly" but the term fits for hell—all of us were ugly down there: in appearance, character, and intent.

During unmerciful torments, I seemed to periodically blink out. One such time, I had a quick thought about, "**My things**!" Immediately I heard a loud, deep, growling voice, worse than I could ever express. I don't know whether it came from inside me, was a demon, or what. "They NEVER—BELONGED—TO—YOU!" it exclaimed.

I thought, "Well, my house, my car, my clothes!" More gruffly and adamantly the voice said something like, "Wait, wait, wait, can't you hear?! They were **NEVER—YOURS**! They were ONLY—IN—YOUR—POSSESSION!! THEY—WERE—NOT—YOURS!!!

ARRIVAL

The only thing that belonged to you was **your SOUL**, and look—what you've done—with that!!!" (Deu.30:19) Time for truth, in hell. "Is that why when you die people say, 'You can't take things with you?'" I thought. Yes! because **THOSE THINGS ARE NOT YOURS!!!**[107]

Think-about-it, God spoke of everything "before" it appeared: heaven, earth, jewels, metals, trees, creatures, us (Gen.1:26-27; Ezk.18:4 souls)! We made things we enjoy, from substances provided by God for Himself and us, to enjoy. Nevertheless, the substance or material of **every thing**, rightfully belongs to Him, the LORD God, the true Owner, the land Lord.

We're supposed to be good stewards over these things; and perhaps be giving[108] lots of them away (give that it might be given unto you). We're supposed to set **our** hearts on things above; our treasure is to be in heaven.[109]

That's right! You've got-it! None of these "things" are ours. The Scripture says, **God** owns the cattle on a thousand hills.[110] The silver and gold are His (Hag.2:8)! The earth is the Lord's and the fullness

25

thereof.[111] It's like reality hits and we hear God say, "Hey baby, that stuff is Mine."[112] Amen.

Everything we've worked hard for, paid for, and claim. Everything we have (including our children) belong to God or, we would not be able to have any of them—we'd have none of them! They are literally simply in our possession.

While I was getting beat, my head was forced sideways. When I happened to look slightly upward, I did see a **particular devil**.

This one was sitting a little elevated from where I was. He looked at me, and I looked at him trying to see if that was "Satan."[113] His posture looked as if filing his nails and indicating, "My work is done—you're here!" *[Note: a thorn in the flesh; the messenger of Satan to buffet; accuse; and wear out the saints (2 Corin. 12:7; Rev. 12:10; Daniel 7:25)]*

It seemed some devils were in the walls,[114] as if sitting on seats with their legs crossed. They weren't laughing, smirking, or jumping in contortions of joy.

Their posture indicated, "Yeah, we got you." They weren't happy or sad they got me, it was like a business—as if they were perhaps, pleased.

*

OUT OF BODY TO HELL

7 ~ **Torments**

1) Being separated from, and absence of God, and His blessed influence

2) Being cognizant of former relationship(s) with the Spirit of God (love, goodness, peace, justice, grace, tenderness, mercies, blessings)

3) Repetitive wistful voices of loved ones from the past, giving warnings before destruction (damnation)

4) The realization of having been surrounded by truths all my earthly life, but failing to give credence to them

5) Realizing I could have avoided hell

6) The sense of "the Bliss"

7) Existing eternally in hell, and fear

8) Experiencing myriads of simultaneous non-stop torments (buffets, 2 Cor. 12:7)

9) Inability to escape

10) Expectation of the worst to come

11) Change of address: "region of the lost;" "district of the condemned"

12) Being reserved for the second death[115]

13) Being excessively hot; vulnerable

14) Existence in hell (its lifestyle, abode, residence, dwelling, home, covering)

15) Having keen knowledge of everything and what would happen to me

16) Feeling excruciating pain and intolerable torments

17) Experiencing **"the truth"** of hell

18) No relief, rescue, charity, remorse, positivity

19) No privacy in hell; thoughts exposed, known, open, displayed

20) Memory of the earth-realm lifestyle

21) Filth and degradation; no downtime

22) Memory of sinful commissions, omissions, and experiencing results

23) The continual "rushed" atmosphere

24) A constant dying (they're killing me!)

25) Sufferings of the always, right now, non-stop, forever, eternity

26) Spending eternity with their father, the Devil[116]

27) Seeing some believers, churchgoers

28) Seeing those who **ignored** the Word of God (the Bible); wouldn't draw near to God;[117] didn't choose life, but death; wouldn't accept Jesus as Lord (His deity); whose works were evil.[118]

29) **Definitions**:

   a) **Death** = Separation from His blessed influence.

   b) **Hades** = region of the lost; an area of the body; a segment of a space; territory; district; includes believers (unprofitable servants, Mat. 25:14, 30; a man's two sons, Mat. 21:28, 30; devils are also believers, James. 2:19; devils know who Jesus is, Mark. 1:24; the evil spirit knows Jesus, Acts 19:15).

   c) **Hell** (Lake; Gehenna, tártaros, II Pet. 2:4) = a place or state of the lost and condemned

   (Rev. 20:15)

30) **Areas and degrees in hell**:

   a) Bars of the pit - Job 17:16
   b) Bottomless pit - Rev. 20:1
   c) Chambers of hell - Prov. 7:27
   d) Depths of hell - Prov. 9:18
   e) Gates of hell - Mat. 16:18
   f) Lower parts of earth Psalm 63:9

g) Lowest hell -   Deut. 32:22
h) Stones of the pit -   Isaiah 14:19
i) Sides of pit -   Is. 14:15; Ez. 32:23
j) Portion with unbelievers   Lk.2:46
k) Be more tolerable for some cities than others - Mat. 10:15, 11:22, 11:24
l) Some will get beat with many stripes, some with few stripes -   Luke 12:47-48

31) **Scripture**:

a) Childhood and youth are vanity -   Eccl. 11:9
b) Blessed if die in Lord -   Rev.14:13
c) Disobedient son (believer) -   Matt. 21:28-30
d) Way seems right, end is death - Proverb 14:12
e) God so loved the world -   John 3:16
f) Rebuke sinners openly -   I Tim. 5:20
g) God didn't appoint us to wrath -   I Thes. 5:9
h) Be unjust, filthy, righteous, holy still–Re.22:11

i) The face of the Lord is against them that do evil - I Peter 3:12

j) It's appointed once to die, then judgment - Hebrews 9:27

k) Some believed, some believed not Acts 28:24; Mark. 16:11, 13

The Lord later informed me that the torments I experienced, were the torments being experienced by some currently in hell, as well as some who'd just died and arrived (even that morning) down there!

For example, some were being tormented relative to their stomachs. To "stomach" something means to bear or tolerate. To be hit in one's stomach, renders a disability or inability to tolerate (or to stomach); therein, making hell all the more intolerable.

Immediately I remembered getting hit in my stomach; and I'm supposed to tell you all—all about it.

*

8 ~ I Came Back

"When she came back I was there; and I saw the impact that it had on her." ~ Floyd ~

I can't tell you how I came back here,[119] I don't know. **I can't say I ascended**; I don't remember that. I don't know if someone just knocked me out, and processed me back here, or what.

I think God scooped[120] me into His loving arms of protection:[121] *"Then the king commanded ... lift Jeremiah the prophet out of the dungeon before he dies (Jer. 38:10)."* All I know is suddenly, it seemed my soul and spirit appeared just outside my bedroom door.

Entering my room, was like a baby being born from the womb and still covered with amniotic fluid– I felt like hell was still all over me. Coming back was an extremely slow process. I felt I was still down in hell and not here: a different space, a different sphere.

I recognized the door I entered, my closet and dresser, but was in dismay as to what I was doing back here and why. Shocked, tired, and numb, I walked like a zombie, and felt like a ghost[122] in outer limits. Here, but **not** here—a weird feeling.

I can't say I was grateful, I can't say I was jubilant. I thought any moment "poof," and I'd be back in hell— you don't get out of hell. This one was TOO REAL this time! I **couldn't run** from this one.

Like walking into your house, I was walking into my body: that stuff, that substance I saw laying over there. To verify where I was, I turned to again see my door, etc. *(Job 3:7,11,26)*.

Simultaneously I climbed backwards, feet first, into my body that was on the bed. The eyes of my body were closed, but my soul and spirit could see everything very clearly. However, I didn't have to look at my body—my perception aligned me straight to it.

I CAME BACK

When my husband gets up before I do, he flops the covers off of him and they fold over onto me. Doing so, leaves an airy pocket that makes me very cold. I've asked him, "Honey, when you get up before I do, will you flop the covers back onto your side so I won't get cold?" Well, he forgets sometimes, and he forgot this particular morning.

Returning from the incinerator of hell, I went from being very hot, to feeling cool, cold, chilly, then very chilly.

"Ooooh, I'm cold," shivering in my sleep. My body's temperature had dropped and upon getting back into it, I experienced an immediate change. I think this airy condition contributed to my waking up (as if it assisted in reversing my heated state). Now, I thank God my husband forgot, and for the ventilation.

Still keenly aware, I knew exactly which room my husband was in, what he was doing, his posture, and which room he was about to go into.

While entering that body, my soul and spirit instructed it, "When he gets ready to pass the door, open your eyes, then call his name." Then, my head merged, and rested, like facing upward in its place. (You **can** control your flesh! I Corinthians 9:27.)

Just as he was about to pass the door, my eyes  popped open, I saw his silhouette and said, "*Floyd.*" To me the call sounded lifeless; but he stopped, turned, and came into the bedroom.

I didn't want him to stand in the doorway or sit on the edge of the bed, I wanted him to get back into that bed, flop those covers back over him, and lay there so I could tell him what just happened to me *(Prov.29:18)*.

I don't talk to my husband like that. We always try to be so polite to each other. I don't say, "Honey you do this and you do that!" but this day was different.

I wanted him to come in there and do those things; but before I could open my mouth, it seemed I heard the voice of God tell him to do those things in that order—I didn't have to say it.

He walked in, got in the bed, flopped those covers back over him, laid there, and did not open his mouth.

OUT OF BODY TO HELL

I was surprised! but, it freed me, to simply say, "I dreamt—I went—to hell."

Later, the Lord indicated to me that the more I talk, the more I wake up, then the more dream I forget. The Lord didn't want me to forget details of the **Experience** before telling my husband everything!

My husband has a phenomenal memory, and being wide awake, he would help me remember details to be included in this "Memoir" *(Revelation 2:11)*.

After my return, I heard the Lord in a voice as many waters[123] say to me, "**You have got to tell them! And they, had bet-ter real-ize it because if they don't—they're going there!!!**"

"Lord, You want **me**—to tell this?! I mean, I'm slow of speech. How am I going to get up there and tell them—there's no way. I wish I had a video camera, or a picture. Lord, if I had a video of what happened in hell maybe then, they would believe[124] me. No-no-no, that's okay" (I didn't want to go back to hell for a video)!

He responded, "**You're My video! You're the picture!**"[125] "But Lord, there's no way—I can't get it across to them like I experienced it!" replied my apprehension. He's saying, "**You—get it out!**"

I believe that word "You," means all of us. We have got to tell others of the realities of hell (and the gospel) To spread God's **whole** Word. The other side of the Bible as well, in love. This is a love message—a LOVE WARNING (Ezekiel 3:19; Acts 20:31).

When I came back, I was sitting on my bed making telephone calls to "tell" a few others what happened. While holding the phone, I noticed it didn't seem real to me.

"This thing is not real!" I looked at my sheets on the bed and said, "These aren't real!" I looked at my carpet, dresser, light fixtures, everything, and confessed, "It's not real—this stuff is not real! Lord, this stuff looks like it would melt![126] They all look like a facade!"

The Lord indicated, "That's it, you're right! I've been trying to tell all of you, all along. It's temporal baby, this stuff is temporal, it **is** going to melt.[127] It's all going to pass away." Then, things began to add up more to me! Even now, apparent things speak to me as temporal.

The spiritual world is the **real** world,[128] and it's immediate! It's right here! A perceptive, spiritual eye[129] is required to view it. Yet, it's also intertwined within that last opened mouth breath[130] (exhale of the spirit, ghost, soul, invisible matter *[Genesis 50:26]*). It's just hidden,[131] all covered up by trees, grass, structures, visible matter.

Our spirits are "**the real us.**" You can't see my spirit[132] because it's covered up by my flesh, this earthy house—it's hidden! The visible are images of the invisible (Colossians 1:15-17). The ultrasound is not the baby, it's the image **of** the baby.

Hell is real! It's a real-real. There's something "true" about hell. It's TRUE there **is** a hell. Jesus has the keys to it (Rev. 1:18)! Heaven is a true, real-real. Jesus lives there (Acts 7:55). Life is a vapor (Ja. 4:14), and earth will burn (2 Peter 3:10).

So many are not thinking about the truths of the reality of hell. Sometimes unintentionally, hell and its torments are played down, not mentioned, skipped over, mocked, or avoided, as if they would disappear.

Consequently when **some** loved ones (young and old) die, their soul submits **downward** to the degradational regions of hell because they would not have made preparation to avoid it.

It doesn't matter how much we love(d) them! Not everybody that dies is saved. They're **NOT** always in "**a-better-place!**" We must inform them **before** they expire. Judgment follows physical death.

OUT OF BODY TO HELL

We intentionally prepare for: college, work, promotions, business trips, major purchases, marriages, increasing a family, vacations, retreats, family reunions, possible health issues, hospital admittance, retirement, estate planning, funerals, etc.

There has **got** to be an intentional preparation for our eternity outside of this worldly sphere. Why?! To examples: 1) because after physical expiration of born-again believers, we celebrate what we call a, "Homegoing Service" to the Lord *(souls with the LORD–2 Cor. 5:8)*. 2) However in like manner, after physical expiration of unbelievers, we celebrate what we call a, "Homegoing Service" as well *(though maybe against our hope, souls go to their father, the devil– John 8:44)*.

Like we purchase physical life and property insurance for our houses, vehicles, land, businesses, etc., we need to accept the spiritual gift of **FULL COVERAGE LIFE** insurance from Jesus Christ on our personal, individual SOULS for eternity *("... sealed with the Holy Spirit of promise ..." Eph. 1:13-14; 2 Cor. 5:5. Everlasting life insurance–John.3:16)*.

∗

9 ~ **Finality**

My experience occurred on the **19**th. I understand the number "**9**" means "**FINALITY**," the unveiling of, deliverance, uncovered. There are 9 fruit, 9 gifts, 9 months commonly for the fruit of the womb, 9 planets, etc.

Some historical, though tragic, events that may surprise you took place on dates including the number "**9**" (e.g., 9/11). We must be aware of possible calculated devices; 2 Corinthians 2:11 states, "Lest Satan should get an advantage of us: for we are **not** ignorant of his devices. Rise beyond Satan's deception!

There is something very **FINAL** about this. These **last** days, **end** times, supernatural moves of God. We'd better wake up and take heed. At the **9**th hour, Jesus cried, "Eloi, Eloi, la ma sabachthani?" In St. John chapter "**19**", Jesus said, "**It is FINISHED**", bowed his head, and gave up the ghost.

IN CONCLUSION, hell is **a place**! It is not an illusion or figment of one's imagination. Things the Bible chronicles, and everything we hear about hell from the **serious** speaker is a reality! Be not deceived!

Hell is not being **taught** as frequently as it used to be and should; consequently, many do not believe in the existence of such a place (abyss); tries to hide.

We must let the Lord use us all. He wants all to go ahead and get busy (Mat. 20:6-7). Let the Holy Ghost in us run loose for use. Stop the, "Oh, you-know-now, sometimes..." (reluctant, hard-headed, stiff-necked, missing-the-mark, appointed timing, season) mentality. Jesus said, after the Holy Ghost comes on us, we'd receive power and be His witnesses in earth.

He said we'd be able to do **greater works** because He was going to His Father (John 14:12). Today, there are a variety of ways for individuals to go into all the world and preach the gospel (Mark 16:15), even from the comfort of home. Therefore chronic pain, disc issues, migraines, arthritis, diabetes, fear, infirmities, conditions, disabilities, missing limbs, hearing problems, speaking limitations, visual obstructions, other medical diagnoses, do not matter compared to **souls** going to the real supernatural hell.

It may cost us! The early Church (Jesus' disciples) suffered much evil: scrutiny, false accusations, family rejection, hatred, beatings persecutions, unmerciful deaths by peers, leadership, animals (Heb.11:35-37; Da.7:25a).

Today, some Christians are losing friends, being bullied, intimidated, arrested, and murdered in cold blood (especially in some other countries), for believing in Jesus, dying to flesh, living holy, spreading the gospel, preaching God's kingdom, etc.

Sin, corruption, immorality is soaring. Strategies are being engineered to eliminate the name, "Jesus"; the word, "God"; the word, "**Church**", etc., from everyday societal communications. His end time **CHURCH** (His saints) is facing "NWO" *(New World Order; Nero)*, its full-circle (e.g., Da.7:25b; John 16:28). (Heb.11:35-38; John 15:18-21; Rev. 6:11, 7:14, 17:6) Nevertheless Jesus also said, *"... the gates of **hell** shall not prevail against it"*—**the Church!** (Mt. 16:18)

I hear God saying,

WHERE ARE MY MARTYRS?!"
of today! *(Rev. 6:9-11, 16:6, 17:6)*

✳

10 ~ **Addendum**

In some sectors, the number **nine (9)** is used as an inverted, reversed, and/or upside down number **six (6)**. Six (6) is the number of man (**666**) (Gen.1:27, 31; Rev.13:18).

Genesis 1:26-27 and verse 31, records that it was the sixth (6th) day when God made and created mankind (male and female).

Goliath was "6" cubits and a span, approximately "9 feet, 9 inches" tall (1 Samuel 17:4).

Nebuchadnezzar the king made and set a gold image in Babylon that measured 60 cubits high by 6 cubits wide, thus 90 feet tall and 6 feet wide. (Dan.3:1).

"Now from the **sixth** hour there was darkness over all the land unto the **ninth** hour." (Mt.27:45-46)

Exodus 32:26 – "Who is on the LORD's side?"
Jos.24:15 – "choose you this day whom you will serve "
1 Kings 18:21 – "How long halt you between two
opinions?" Matthew 6:24 - "No one can serve two (2) masters ... you cannot serve God and mammon." ✳

11 ~ **Questions & Answers**

Allow me to state it was not that, had I died, I would have gone to hell (see below).

QUESTION 1: Some have asked **why** I think this experience happened to me.

Answer 1a: After I came back, I heard God say, "**You have got to tell them.**[133] **And they had bet-ter real-ize it because if they don't—they're going there!!!**" Número uno; the main answer.

1b: Some said they think because God knew He could count on me to get it out.

1c: My mother said she knows why, "Because God knows that you would tell other people. That you would spread the news. He knew you would tell this!"

1d: My personal answer: I believe I was allowed to experience hell so I could come back and inform and warn people[134] that hell is a real place, and to avoid it!

To unveil, reveal, uncover, expose, make visible, bring to focus, light, sight, bring to acceptance of, to show some, and help others to **know** it exists for real! To tell you on hell—it is a REAL PLACE! Many in this generation do not believe there is such a place as hell.

1e: My <u>Scriptural answer</u>: "... in weariness and toil, in sleeplessness often, in hunger and thirst, in fastings often, in cold and nakedness—besides the other things, what comes upon me daily: my deep concern for all the churches" (2 Cor. 11:27-28).

<u>QUESTION 2</u>: Some have asked, what I think the reason was for me seeing clergy men and women, churchgoers, etc., going to hell?

Answer 2a: I think the clergy, laity, etc., I saw simply represent "the office, positions, or situations" of some who "**eternally exist**" in hell (right now) for various commissions/omissions of sin.

2b: I think the clergy I saw simply represent some (not all) clergy, who are currently, spiritually "**on the pathway**" (1 Co. 9:27) to hell and will go there unless

Q&As

they truly repent from unrighteousness,[135] self-righteousness, lack of sincere love for the brethren (and "called" sisteren), insecurities among each other as opposed to the prayer of Jesus "that they all may be one" (John 17:21), etc.

2c: Because people want to hear from someone they think knows what they're talking about, some sarcastically ask, "**How can you tell me something unless you've been there?**"

Miraculously after hearing this experience, it became apparent that some **did** go to hell with me, but **vicariously**. To my surprise, some are saying things like, *"As you were speaking, I was there! I went with you in hell. I saw what you were talking about."* Thus **vicariously, they were there** and comprehended hell.

Even more, we're seeking God and **His** will, praying effectually, fervently, examining ourselves, studying,[136] forgiving, etc., to be a greater witness. Thank God for the pure river of water of life (Rev. 22:1-4).

2d: Seeing the others is also indicative of some who are experiencing "personal" God-given encounters, thus are **able to relate** to my excursion. E.g., a woman of another State who truly loves the Lord, dreamed friends in heaven couldn't find her there because "she" was **in hell**.

2e: Seeing other clergy also equates to forms of "partnership" in ministerial support to help get this message of hell out to as many souls as possible that they may avoid it. **Some perceived** this journey and its importance in this hour.

QUESTION 3: Some of my colleagues have asked, "Did you see **me** there?" "Was **I** one of the ones you saw going to hell?"

Answer 3: To the ones who have asked this question I had to say, "Yes," because I did see them. But the explanation to, or interpretation of, this question is a detailed, revelatory "**RHEMA**" answer:

If I had seen only multitudes of people I did **not** know, I would not have known their capacity, position, who they were, or what they stood for in this life; however, because I saw colleagues, people I know of and recognized, I was able to distinguish their capacities in life, what **they** stand for—they represented various "**ministerial offices.**"

The "ministerial offices" represent some people in those capacities who are **NOT living up to God's "Standard."** (2 Co. 11:13) It's a *love warning (Ez. 3:19)* from the Father of lights.

To reiterate, in order to say, "I saw many pastors, preachers, teachers, evangelists, apostles, bishops, prophets, deacons, laity, church goers, believers, relatives, all of us, whatever we call ourselves," I had to **recognize** those offices.

It was not that each individual soul of my colleagues were, or are, going to hell (though it truly depends on which side of the fence one is on).

QUESTION 4: Some wonder "**why**" they dream and/or are visionaries, and "what" to do with the insight.

Answer 4a: Ask the Lord God for its interpretation. Receive His answer, and possible confirmation(s). Sometimes He allows this to instill confidence in you, until **YOU** recognize that He plans to **use** the ability (potential) He's vested **in** you.

God is raising many, and revealing experiences across the universe to warn[137] this generation of things to come.[138] Things are manifesting. The Deity of Christ must faithfully be acknowledged.

The bottom line is, if we are NOT living **holy**, we need to examine our hearts, reevaluate our motives, search the Scriptures, see if we're in the faith, make sure Jesus is our first love, and be living epistles. God loves us, this is why **He reveals His secret**(s).

The purpose of this book is not to frighten anyone. It is to unveil, expose and inform some (as best I can) of the description of **the place** of hell as I experienced it. I don't feel I have time; but, to do this immediately. **Behold, I have told you**.

Q&As

TO THE ANGELS OF THE CHURCHES:

"... the Lord said to him ... Utterly slay old and young men, maidens and little children and women; but do not come near anyone on whom is the mark; **and begin at My sanctuary**. So they began with the elders who were before the temple." *(Ezek.9:4,6)*

"Therefore take **heed** to yourselves and to all the flock, among which the Holy Spirit has made **you** overseers, to **shepherd the church of God** which He purchased with His own blood." *(Acts 20:28)*

"In the latter days you will understand it perfectly. I have not sent these prophets, yet they ran. I have not spoken to them, yet they prophesied." *(Jer.23:20b-21)*

"... let not many of you become teachers, knowing that we shall receive a **stricter judgment**. *(James 3:1)*

"... And he said to Him, 'Lord; ...; You know that I love You.' Jesus said to him, 'Feed **My sheep** ...' (St.Jn. 21:17b)

✳

12 ~ **Definitions**

"For the time has come for judgment to begin at the house of God ..." *(I Peter 4:17)*

believer - in particular, possessing the distinguishing characteristic of a Christian; belief, trust, persuasion, confidence with assent to faith in Christ or the Gospel.

hell – spirit realm of evil, suffering; fire under earth.

out of body – sensation of floating outside of one's body with ability to view it and area from distance.

righteous - conformable to right, those who are just, honest, obedient to God's laws.

sinner - miss the way, heinous, unjust, practicing deviant, to endanger, incur guilt, off target, breach civil law, bearing blame, fault, short of God's standard.

unbeliever - not worthy of confidence, untrustworthy, not believing, an infidel.

ungodly - godless; without fear and reverence of God; outwardly religious but actively practicing the opposite of what the fear of God demands; immoral and impious behavior (pretenders).

wicked - law breaker, liable to punishment, poorly regulated, guilty of violating social rights, oppress the righteous, sinful, godless, vicious, guilty, they hate the Lord. ✽

57

13 ~ God's Word to Us

"Surely the Lord God does nothing, Unless **He reveals His secret** to His servants the prophets. A lion has roared! Who will not fear? The Lord God has spoken! Who can but prophesy?" *(Amos 3:7-8)*

"And on some have compassion, making a distinction; but others save with fear, pulling them **out of the fire** hating even the garment defiled by the flesh." (Ju. 22-23)

"And fear not them which kill the body, but are not able to kill the soul: but rather fear Him which is able to destroy both **soul and body in hell**." *(St. Matt. 10:28)*

"Behold, all souls are Mine; as the soul of the father, so also the soul of the son is Mine: **the soul that sins, it shall die**." *(Ezekiel 18:4)*

"Do you not know that the **unrighteous will not inherit the kingdom of God**? Do not be deceived. Neither fornicators, nor idolaters, nor adulterers, nor homosexuals, nor sodomites, nor thieves, nor covetous, nor drunkards, nor revilers, nor extortioners will inherit the kingdom of God." *(1 Corinthians. 6:9-10)*

13b ~ **God's Word to Us** *(cont'd)*

"Jesus ... taking vengeance on them that know not God, and that **obey not the gospel** of our Lord Jesus Christ: who shall be punished with everlasting destruction from the presence of the Lord " *(2 Thes. 1:7-9)*

"Therefore **hell hath enlarge** herself, and opened her mouth without measure ..." *(Isaiah 5:14)*

"Yet thou shalt be brought **down to hell**, to the sides of the pit. They that see thee shall narrowly look upon thee ..." *(Isaiah 14:15-16)*

"And the **devil that deceived them** was cast into the lake of fire and brimstone, where the beast and the false prophet are, and shall be tormented day and night for ever and ever. And **death and hell** were cast into the lake of fire. This is the second death." *(Rev. 20:10, 14)*

"He who has an ear, let him hear what the **Spirit says to the churches**. He who overcomes shall not be hurt by the second death." *(Revelation 2:11)*

"... And I knew such a man, (whether in the body, or **out of the body**, I cannot tell: God knoweth) How that he was caught up into paradise and heard unspeakable words, ..." *(2 Corin. 12:3-4)* ✶

14 ~ Epilogue

He came to His own, and His own received Him not; but as many as received Him, to them gave He power *(John 1:11-12)*.

~Oh Jerusalem, Jerusalem, how often I *(Jesus)* would have gathered your children and shielded them *(Lk.13:34)*.

~What I tell you in darkness, that speak in light; and, what you hear in the ear, that preach on the housetops. And do not fear them who kill the body but cannot kill the soul *(Matthew 10:27-28a)*.

~We wrestle not against flesh and blood, but against principalities, powers, the rulers of darkness of this world, spiritual wickedness in high places; take the whole armor of God and stand *(Ephesians 6:12)*!

~Be not deceived; God is not mocked *(Galatians 6:7)*.

If disarray in this earth realm today concerns you: hostile crimes, resentment, insecurities, political malfeasance, wars, bullies, animal attacks, the unknown, families taking frustrations out on each other; then realize the fact that, if this earth can have such detrimental behavior—surely, a REAL HELL below must actually exist!

Therefore, some had better choose to get their **soul's** saved right now because, if death were to suddenly knock at their physical, personal, door *(of life)* and

14b ~ **Epilogue** *(cont'd)*

greet them with a message from be-low, saying, "**HEL-LO!**" *(Hell-is-low; thus, hell—lo.)* They will **NOT** be better off!!!"

To eternally exist in hell would be the laying bare of one's soul to an overwhelming collection of vicious waste, a thrash dump site, a landfill of what's unwanted, thrown out, eliminated, bad, exiled. One's soul would be exposed among inescapable schizophrenia. To reside in hell would be worse than being sentenced to death row in the highest maximum security prison *(camp)*.

Hell is inclusive of every unrepentant soul since the beginning of humankind. E.g.: cruel, barbaric, ruthless kings, emperors, presidents; inhumane rulers; selfish lovers of worldly riches; the uncivilized, wicked, immoral, unrighteous, ignorant; the devil, beast, and false prophet.

Any sinner who goes to hell, might find themselves having to interface with other souls they never thought they'd see again and/or meet from history. I implore everyone who is not saved: It would behoove you to, *"Choose you this day who you will serve!" (Jos.24:15)*

Right now, souls breathing in this world are either spiritually alive or spiritually dead; but, when there is no more time? *(Rev. 10:6)* like: when time is up? all over? done? gone? ended? fini?! *(Jn.19:30)* Unrepentant souls shall remain in their same state; the door will be shut; choices solidified; judgment *(Mt. 25:10)*.✶

15 ~ **Pray Aloud**

Lord Jesus, You love me so deeply, help me pray: "I believe You are the Son of God Who took away the sin of the world. I believe God raised You from the dead and You're in heaven helping me right now. I repent.

Please forgive me of all sins I've committed and omitted. Come into my life—make me a new creature—I want to be saved. I accept You as Lord over my life. I have faith in God through You. Teach me Lord so I will spiritually grow. Fill me with the Holy Ghost so I can do God's will. Thank You so much! In Your name, Jesus, I pray. Amen." *(Romans 10:9-10)*

If you prayed this or similar prayer, believing with all your heart, tell a Christian who you respect that you just prayed to the Lord Jesus to receive salvation.

On this _____ day of _____, 20_____; I, _____, became a brand new creature in Christ Jesus. I am born again, will turn away from sin, get baptized as soon as I can, will study the Bible, attend church, and do God's will. Praise You Lord!

_____*(signature)* ✶

16 ~ **Endnotes**

1. Numbers 12:6; St. Matthew 10:26-27
2. II Corinthians 12:1
3. Habakkuk 2:2-3
4. I Kings 19:12; St. John 6:44
5. James 4:8
6. Ezekiel 3:22-24
7. Prov. 31:10-12; II Tim. 2:14-16; I Cor. 9:26-27
8. Ecclesiastes 12:10-11
9. 2 Timothy 3:5; St. Matthew 7:19-23
10. Ezekiel 8:6-18, 11:2-3, 13:1-4; I Samuel 2:22-25; St. Matthew 7:3-6, 25:41-46;
11. II Peter 3:11
12. Job 34:14-15; St. Matthew 15:13-14
13. Psalm 50:4-5; St. Matthew 13:41-42
14. St. Matthew 2:2, 24:27; Revelation 16:12
15. St. Matthew 13:30
16. Isaiah 14:19
17. Isaiah 13:10; Ezekiel 32:7-8
18. Psalm 40:2; II Peter 2:4
19. Proverb 1:24-27
20. Mt. 25: 41, 46; I Thess. 5:2-4; Rev. 10:6, 22:11

21. St. John 15:6
22. Isaiah 64:6; Psalm 78:49
23. St. Matthew 25:44-46
24. St. Matthew 6:24
25. St. Matthew 7:22
26. St. Matthew 7:21-23; Psalm 6:8
27. St. Matthew 23:6; Isaiah 14:11
28. St. Matthew 7:21-22
29. Revelation 20:11-12
30. St. Matthew 23:4-6, 23:23-25, 24:24-25
31. Revelation 2:23; Ezekiel 9:1-11; St. Luke 16:13
32. Ezekiel 9:1-11; St. Luke 16:13
33. St. Matthew 16:18
34. Deuteronomy 30:19
35. Psalm 139:8
36. Proverbs 5:5, 9:18; Mt. 13a;26-30, 38-43, 49-51
37. Is.66:15-16, 24; Lk.16:24; Mt. 5:22; Rev.20:10-15
38. St. Matthew 16:18
39. Isaiah 14:19
40. Jude 6
41. Isaiah 14:15
42. Proverb 1:27

43. Psalm 9:17
44. St. Matthew 23:13-15; I Corinthians 9:27
45. Genesis 3:22; I Corinthians 13:12; St. Luke 16:23
46. I Corinthians 13:13; St. John 6:70, 8:44;
    Acts 13:10; 1 John 3:10; I Samuel 2:22
47. II Thessalonians 1:8
48. Acts 3:23; Jeremiah 23:22, 26
49. Isaiah 49:1; Jeremiah 29:19
50. Ezekiel 33:31
51. Jeremiah 13:11, 23:24; Zechariah 7:13-14
52. Acts 18:10; St. John 14:17-18
53. St. Matthew 28:20
54. Hebrews 10:7, 13:5-6; St. John 5:38-41
55. Revelation 1:3, 2:11
56. Hosea 4:6
57. James 4:13-14
58. Isaiah 13:11
59. I Kings 19:12-13
60. Revelation 22:7, 11-13, 16, 20; Jeremiah 22:23
61. St. John 17:3; 3:16
62. St. John 21:15-17
63. St. John 19:25-27

64. St. John 14:15
65. Hebrews 11:6
66. St. Mark 2:3-5
67. Prov. 1:12, 2:18, 7:27; Ps.18:5; Jer. 38:9
68. Ezekiel 9:6; Jeremiah 46:28
69. Isaiah 13:16
70. Jeremiah 9:21-22
71. Ezekiel 31:17
72. Revelation 21:8
73. I Samuel 28:14; St. Luke 16:23
74. Jeremiah 38:6
75. St. Matthew 22:13
76. St. Matthew 22:13; St. Luke 16:23
77. Revelation 1:12
78. Revelation 20:14-15
79. Isaiah 14:11, 66:24
80. Isaiah 14:9
81. Lev. 16:21-22; St. Mt. 27:20; I Pe. 2:24; Rev. 5:9
82. St. Mark 8:36-37; Jeremiah 23:21-23, 29:9
83. I Samuel 28:11-15
84. St. Matthew 18:34
85. Psalm 18:17

86. Daniel 8:7
87. Jeremiah 23:29, 29:19
88. Judges 5:26-27, Amos 9:1
89. I John 4:18
90. Isaiah 14:11; Jeremiah 23:29
91. St. Matthew 13:42
92. St. Luke 16:26
93. Isaiah 5:14
94. Hebrews 2:2-3; St. John 8:41, 44
95. I Samuel 28:7-14; Acts 13:6-11
96. Acts 16:16-18
97. Galatians 5:17-21
98. I Samuel 15:23; Romans 1:24-32; 2 Timothy 3:2
99. St. Matthew 5:28-30
100. Psalm 50:17; II Timothy 3:1-4
101. Ephesians 2:2-3
102. II Corinthians 2:11; I Peter 5:8
103. St. Luke 16:23; Acts 1:9-10; II Corinthians 12:2
104. Ephesians 4:8
105. Revelation 20:10
106. Mt.12:32, 13:38b-42, 50; Jn.8:44-45; Rev.16:10-11
107. Job 1:4; I Timothy 6:7

108. St. Luke 6:38
109. St. Matthew 6:19-20
110. Psalm 50:10-11
111. Psalm 24:1-2
112. Psalm 50:12
113. Job 1:7; Isaiah 14:12-17; Revelation 20:10
114. Isaiah 14:9-10, 19; II Peter 2:4
115. Revelation 20:14
116. St. John 8:44
117. James 4:8
118. I John 3:12; Revelation 2:23, 20:12
119. Job 33:18
120. Jeremiah 38:10
121. Psalm 18:17-19, 29:7, 40:2-3; Jeremiah 37:16-17
122. Psalm 39:5-6; Job 3:7,11,26; Mt.7:19-23
123. Psalm 18:13, 29:3-9; Job 37:1-5
124. St. Mark 16:9-14; St. Luke 16:29-30
125. II Corinthians 3:3; Revelation 1:19
126. II Peter 3:10-11
127. II Peter 2:3:7, 10-12
128. Hebrews 11:3
129. II Kings 6:16-17

130. St. Lk. 16:22-23; II Cor. 5:8; Acts 7:59; Jn.19:30
131. St. Matthew 10:26; Colossians 1:16
132. I Corinthians 15:44; Prov. 20:27, Eccl. 12:7
133. Amos 3:7-8; I Peter 5:20; Revelation 10:11
134. Job 33:22-24; Rev. 2:4, 10:9-11, 22:16; Hab. 2:2-3
135. I Sam. 2:22; Ezek. 8:6-18, 33:31; Eccl. 12:14; Ps. 78:36, 41; II Tim. 3:1-5
136. II Corinthians 13:5, II Timothy 2:15
137. Ezekiel 3:16-21; Revelation 2:4
138. Revelation 4:1, 20:12-15

*

17 ~ Notes

17b ~ **Notes** *(cont'd)*

✳

18 ~ About the Author

Beverly J. Williams, DM, is an American Christian; Ordained and Associate Minister; gifted Bible Teacher; twice ABA Approved & Certified Paralegal; Nonfiction Christian Author; and a media producer *(books, audio media, former TV ministry)*.

She has earned several academic and ministerial collegiate degrees, including a Bachelor of Science in Organizational Leadership, a Master's in Bible Subjects, and a Doctor of Ministry. Though she is an intermittent collegiate Bible student, she nevertheless, credits her inmost learning to intimacy with the Holy Ghost, and personal, in-depth, Bible study.

Her gift in Bible teaching afforded her the opportunity to teach and demonstrate the gospel of Christ Jesus in various platforms, to miscellaneous cultures, and counsel many. To date, her clear, concise style, simplifies comprehension for younger generations and the more mature. Her instinctive nuances contribute to her ability to perceive subtle, nondisclosed details.

She is united in holy matrimony to her beloved husband, Floyd W. Williams, Sr., PhD; also a graduate of several academic universities and ministerial seminaries, a retired Contractor, an Associate Pastor, and a servant-leader in communities known as an humble man of integrity.

They respond to the clarion call of God through their multifaceted Ministry of 45+ years to the local and universal Church, communities, and various forms of ministry. Since 1996 Beverly has authored: *Faith by The Word; Please Let Me Be Who I Am; Pathway to Hell; He Reveals His Secret; and El Revela Su Secreto.* See her forthcoming publications.

With utmost reverential esteem, she states she deeply loves the Lord God, and is humbly grateful to have been chosen by Him. ✷

19 ~ Literary, Digital, Media

1-Faith by The Word *(5.25 x 3.5)* — paperback []
2-Faith by The Word *(35 min.)* — audiobook []
3-Please Let Me be Who I AM *(5.25 x 3.5)* — paperback []
4-Please Let Me be Who I AM *(34 min.)* — audiobook []
5-Pathway to Hell *(length 1.5 hour)* — dvd []
6-He Reveals His Secret *(5.25 x 3.5; english)* — paperback []
7-El Revela Su Secreto *(5.25 x 3.5; spanish)* — paperback []
8-Out of Body to Hell *(5 x 8; english)* — paperback []
9-Out of Body to Hell *(70 min.; english)* — audiobook []
10-Fuera del Cuerpo al Infierno *(5 x 8; spanish)* — paperback []
11-Fuera del Cuerpo al Infierno *(68 min; spanish)* — audiobook[]

"Out of Body to Hell" paperback, eBook, and audiobooks are from the internationally distributed book, "He Reveals His Secret" (and "El Revela Su Secreto" in Spanish). Other media by Floyd W. & Beverly J. Williams may be in bookstores, online, video channels, webpage(s), libraries. Please spread the word. Thank you. To God be all the glory!

"THANK YOU FOR READING. IF YOU'D LIKE, FEEL FREE TO LEAVE AN HONEST BOOK REVIEW ON THE BOOK PLATFORM(S) OF YOUR CHOICE—IT WILL HELP OTHERS. BLESSINGS TO YOU AND YOURS." ✷

20 ~ Scan QR Code

Ministers of the Gospel, Inc.
www.ms7.com

Use a QR reader or smartphone:

Open camera, hover over QR Code, click pop-up link, explore www.ms7.com for updates on paperbacks, eBooks, audiobooks, online, video channels, webpage(s), libraries, etc.

Organizations, individuals: Add to your spiritual resources—share with churches, conferences, Bible studies, missionaries, ministries, evangelistic teams, seminaries, universities, bookstores, family gatherings, youth camps, teenage clubs, groups young and elderly, any interested in eschatology, afterlife, judgment day, souls, hell.

Christians: Recognize our enemies! The third part of the stars of heaven that were cast to the earth *(Rev.13:4)*. Principalities, powers, rulers of the darkness of this world, spiritual wickedness in high places *(Eph.6:12)*. God cast some of the sinful 3rd angels down to Tartarus, delivering them into chains of darkness, to be reserved till judgment *(2 Pet.2:4)*. The spirit of error *(I Jn.4:6)*. Cain was of the wicked one *(1 Jn.3:12)*. Workers of iniquity *(Mt.7:23)*. The tares are of the enemy *(Jn.8:44)*. Every spirit that confesses not that Jesus Christ is come in the flesh, that spirit of antichrist *(1 Jn.4:3)*.

✳   IXΘYE